The author was born towards the end of World War II to Middle Eastern Christian parents in the historical Assyrian heartland. His family is denominationally Catholic and liturgically Syriac, an offshoot of the Church of Antioch that was founded by Saint Peter, one of the twelve disciples of Jesus.

In his boyhood and during early primary school, he had served in the Church as an altar boy and certainly was destined to become a deacon. However, his family moved to another town and this caused his church involvement to change.

His whole life, he was not fully Christian but most times a churchgoer with no deep conversance with the Holy Scriptures. This was the norm for most of his generation due to cultural impact, except for those close to or relative to clerics who managed to get acquainted with parts of the scriptures. His parents, especially his father, instilled in him the high moral codes that would remain with him throughout his whole life—always modest and always honest.

In the early 1970s, the author ordered his first copy of the Holy Bible via his priest, written in the common language of the land. He started from the first cover then the Book of Genesis but going through the first chapter, he found it difficult to grasp what he read; it was a formidable task to scale. In later years, he realised that a beginner must not start reading the whole Bible from cover to cover but by selecting easier books of the Bible to digest and tune with the text. Once acquainted with some knowledge of the Bible, then go for the whole Bible from cover to cover.

In the late 1970s, he departed from his town of birth to obtain western education and upgrade his postgraduate degree, and it was then that his Christian sphere started to widen with links to both Catholic Chaplaincies and Christian Unions. He had a good circle of Christian friends and it continued even after he had finished his courses and went into academic life in the 1980s, 1990s and beyond. Now, his faith in Jesus is sealed and complete.

To the memory of my father, Habash Anton, and my mother, Farida Yacob, for instilling in me the love and fear of God.

George Habash

I Am a Christian

AUSTIN MACAULEY PUBLISHERS™
LONDON • CAMBRIDGE • NEW YORK • SHARJAH

Copyright © George Habash (2021)

The right of George Habash to be identified as author of this work has been asserted by the author in accordance with section 77 and 78 of the Copyright, Designs and Patents Act 1988.

All rights reserved. No part of this publication may be reproduced, stored in a retrieval system, or transmitted in any form or by any means, electronic, mechanical, photocopying, recording, or otherwise, without the prior permission of the publishers.

Any person who commits any unauthorised act in relation to this publication may be liable to criminal prosecution and civil claims for damages.

A CIP catalogue record for this title is available from the British Library.

ISBN 9781528911511 (Paperback)
ISBN 9781398427778 (ePub e-book)

www.austinmacauley.com

First Published (2021)
Austin Macauley Publishers Ltd
25 Canada Square
Canary Wharf
London
E14 5LQ

This work did not spring out from anything and was hardly dependent on my own wit and would not have been possible without the contributions, efforts, kindness and love of many others.

Sincere thanks are given to my immediate family; Idris, Ameen, Anees, Messon, Ismail, Mauona (deceased), Hosni and Malgorzata. Friends and acquaintances through the years who have an indelible impact. Acknowledgement of special thanks and gratitude are extended to my longtime friends and colleagues, especially Arnold J Smith and John R Helliwell for years of academic and post-academic collaboration and friendship.

I thank many Christian ministries for their literature, many Christian television channels and many Christian preachers/ teachers on those channels who fed me with 'The Word of God' on a daily basis.

Finally, I exalt and honour the noble people of my hometown, Baretly, near the historic Nineveh in the Assyrian heartland.

I Am a Christian

What does it mean?

I believe in Jesus Christ (the Christ), prophesied in the Old Testament and revealed in the New Testament. I follow him in faith and work and believe the Gospel and I am saved by his sacrifice on the cross.

Anyone can become Christian as is pointed out in Acts 2:38: "Repent and be baptised, every one of you, in the name of Jesus Christ so that your sins may be forgiven. And you will receive the gift of the Holy Spirit."

What Is Christianity?

Christianity is a faith that God became man in Jesus Christ (through Virgin Mary by the power of the Holy Spirit) to redeem the human race (all humanity) from mortal sin inherited from Adam and Eve.

It affirms that Jesus Christ died by shedding his blood on the Cross for the atonement of humanity's sins as an act of love. It affirms that Jesus Christ was resurrected to life as an act of power. It affirms that Jesus Christ ascended to the Father. It affirms that Jesus Christ sent his Holy Spirit to his church. And it affirms that Jesus Christ will come again (the second coming) in power and majesty before the final judgement. Christianity is a second Temple Movement started by Jesus Christ.

In a nutshell, any man or woman cannot meet God's standard, because we fall short of his glory and a Saviour (Jesus Christ) is the mediator between us and God – this is Christianity.

The First Church

Prior to Pentecost day and specifically on Ascension Day, the believers numbered just about 120 believers (those in the open or secret) who later assembled in the upper room in Jerusalem to select a replacement for Judas Iscariot (Acts 1:15). On Pentecost day, some ten days later in the same upper room, the Holy Spirit gave them utterance and those were the beginnings of the early Church. About 3,000 people came to faith in Christ on that day. That was the first Sunday Christian gathering for worship.

Pentecost in Greek or Shavuot in Hebrew meant two things. The first, it was not many races who gathered that day but one universal faith and one church. The second was to go out and preach the gospel to the end of the earth.

On Pentecost day, some fifteen days after the resurrection, Jesus handed his ministry to the church when he sent the Holy Spirit with a gift of power on that gathering. The church was born and continues to exist on this day to reach out for the unreached worldwide. Mary, the mother of Jesus, was with the disciples and part of the church.

The Nicene Creed is the conclusion of the Council of Nicaea in 325 AD that formulated the profession of the Christian faith and in some churches can be recited individually (I believe) or collectively (we believe). A Christian church or a Christian individual must adhere to these articles of faith. There are three main beliefs represented in the first three paragraphs (here is the Catholic version):

"I believe in one God, the Father almighty, maker of heaven and earth, of all things visible and invisible.

"I believe in one Lord Jesus Christ, the only begotten Son of God, born of the Father before all ages. God from God, Light from Light, true God from true God, begotten, not made, consubstantial with the Father; through him, all things were made.

"For us men and for our salvation, he came down from heaven, and by the Holy Spirit was incarnate of the Virgin Mary, and became man.

"For our sake, he was crucified under Pontius Pilate, he suffered death and was buried, and rose again on the third day in accordance with the Scriptures.

"He ascended into heaven and is seated at the right hand of the Father. He will come again in glory to judge the living and the dead and his kingdom will have no end.

"I believe in the Holy Spirit, the Lord, the giver of life, who proceeds from the Father and the Son, who with the Father and the Son is adored and glorified, who has spoken through the prophets.

"I believe in one, holy, catholic and apostolic Church.

"I confess one baptism for the forgiveness of sins and

"I look forward to the resurrection of the dead and the life of the world to come. Amen."

The Core Bible Verses

All the following Bible verses are taken from NIV version issue 1983 and restricted to the Hebrew Bible only. Later in the book, a few selected verses of the New Testament will be shown.

"In the beginning God created the heavens and the earth." (Genesis 1:1).

"Let there be light, and there was light." (Genesis 1:3).

"So God created man in his own image, in the image of God he created him; male and female he created them." (Genesis 1:27).

"For this reason a man will leave his father and mother and be united to his wife, and they will become one flesh." (Genesis 2:24).

"I will make you into a great nation and I will bless you; I will make your name great and you will be a blessing.

"I will bless those who bless you, and whoever curses you I will curse; and all peoples on earth will be blessed through you." (Genesis 12:2–3).

"To your descendants I give this land, from the river of Egypt to the great river, the Euphrates." (Genesis 15:18).

"…a land flowing with milk and honey…" (Exodus 3:8).

"The Lord is slow to anger, abounding in love and forgiving sin and rebellion…" (Numbers 14:18).

"Hear, O Israel, The Lord our God, the Lord is one. Love the Lord your God with all your heart and with all your soul and with all your strength." (Deuteronomy 6:4–5).

"…man does not live on bread alone but on every word that comes from the mouth of the Lord." (Deuteronomy 8:3).

"…I will never leave you or forsake you." (Joshua 1:5).

"…Where you go I will go, and where you stay I will stay. Your people will be my people and your God my God.

Where you die I will die, and there I will be buried…" (Ruth 1:16–17).

"If my people, who are called by my name, will humble themselves and pray and seek my face and turn from their wicked ways, then I will hear from heaven and will forgive their sin and will heal their land." (2 Chronicles 7:14).

"Naked I came from my mother's womb, and naked I shall depart. The Lord gave and the Lord has taken away; may the name of the Lord be praised." (Job 1:21).

"He spreads out the northern skies over empty space; he suspends the earth over nothing." (Job 26:7).

"By the rivers of Babylon we sat and wept when we remembered Zion." (Psalm 137:1).

"I praise you because I am fearfully and wonderfully made…" (Psalm 139:14).

"Let everything that has breath praise the Lord. Praise the Lord." (Psalm 150:6).

"The fear of the Lord is the beginning of knowledge…" (Proverbs 1:7)

"What has been will be again, what has been done will be done again; there is nothing new under the sun." (Ecclesiastes 1:9).

"I am a rose of Sharon, a lily of the valleys." (Song of Songs 2:1).

"Therefore the Lord himself will give you a sign: The virgin will be with child and will give birth to a son, and will call him Immanuel." (Isaiah 7:14).

"The people walking in darkness have seen a great light; on those living in the land of the shadow of death a light has dawned." (Isaiah 9:2).

"For to us a child is born, to us a son is given, and the government will be on his shoulders. And he will be called Wonderful Counsellor, Mighty God, Everlasting Father, Prince of Peace." (Isaiah 9:6).

"The wolf will live with the lamb, the leopard will lie down with the goat, the calf and the lion and yearling together; and a little child will lead them." (Isaiah 11:6).

"They will neither harm nor destroy on all my holy mountain, for the earth will be full of the knowledge of the Lord as the waters cover the sea." (Isaiah 11:9).

"…but those who hope in the Lord will renew their strength. They will soar on wings like eagles; they will run and not grow weary, they will walk and not be faint." (Isaiah 40:31).

"…I am the first and I am the last; apart from me there is no God." (Isaiah 44:6).

"…Before me every knee will bow; by me every tongue will swear." (Isaiah 45:23).

"…Though the mountains be shaken and the hills be removed, yet my unfailing love for you will not be shaken nor my covenant of peace be removed…" (Isaiah 54:10).

"You will go out in joy and be led forth in peace; the mountains and hills will burst into song before you, and all the trees of the field will clap their hands." (Isaiah 55:12).

"Before I formed you in the womb I knew you, before you were born I set you apart; I appointed you as a prophet to the nations." (Jeremiah 1:5).

"I will give them an undivided heart and put a new spirit in them; I will remove from them their heart of stone and give them a heart of flesh. Then they will follow my decrees and be careful to keep my laws. They will be my people, and I will be their God." (Ezekiel 11:19–20).

"For every living soul belongs to me, the father as well as the son – both alike belong to me. The soul who sins is the one who will die." (Ezekiel 18:4).

"The righteousness of the righteous man will be credited to him, and the wickedness of the wicked will be charged against him." (Ezekiel 18:20).

"…The lowly will be exalted and the exalted will be brought low." (Ezekiel 21:26).

"…my people are destroyed from lack of knowledge…" (Hosea 4:6).

"Rend your heart and not your garments. Return to the Lord your God, for he is gracious and compassionate, slow to anger and abounding in love, and he relents from sending calamity." (Joel 2:13).

"…I will pour out my Spirit on all people. Your sons and daughters will prophesy, your old men will dream dreams, your young men will see visions…" (Joel 2:28).

"And anyone who calls on the name of the Lord will be saved…" (Joel 2:32).

"My people, what have I done to you? How have I burdened you? Answer me?" (Micah 6:3).

"He has showed you, O man, what is good. And what does the Lord require of you? To act justly and to love mercy and to walk humbly with your God." (Micah 6:8).

"For the earth will be filled with the knowledge of the glory of the Lord, as the waters cover the sea." (Habakkuk 2:14).

"…'Return to me,' declares the Lord Almighty, 'and I will return to you,' says the Lord Almighty." (Zechariah 1:3).

"…'Not by might nor by power, but by my Spirit,' says the Lord Almighty." (Zechariah 4:6).

"Strike the shepherd, and the sheep will be scattered…" (Zechariah 13:7–8).

"…My name will be great among the nations, from the rising to the setting of the sun…" (Malachi 1:11).

"I the Lord do not change…Return to me, and I will return to you…" (Malachi 3:6–7).

The Ten Commandment (Decalogue)

The Ten Commandments given to Moses (and to the Israelites) on Mount Sinai, written on two tablets of stone, inscribed by the finger of God (on both sides, front and back) with the law and commands of God are written for their instruction are found in Exodus 20:1–17:

> "I am the Lord your God, who brought you out of Egypt, out of the land of slavery. You shall have no other gods before me.
>
> "You shall not take for yourself an idol in the form of anything in heaven above or on the earth below. You shall not bow down to them or worship them; for I, the Lord your God, am a jealous God, punishing the children for the sin of the fathers to the third and fourth generation of those who hate me, but showing love to thousands who love me and keep my commandments.
>
> "You shall not misuse the name of the Lord your God, for the Lord will not hold anyone guiltless who misuses his name.
>
> "Remember the Sabbath day by keeping it holy. Six days you shall labour and do all your work, but the seventh day is a Sabbath to the Lord your God. On it you shall not do any work, neither you, nor your son or daughter, nor your manservant or maidservant, nor your animals, nor the alien within your gates."

For in six days, the Lord made the heavens and earth, the sea, and all that is in them, but he rested on the seventh day. Therefore, the Lord blessed the Sabbath day and made it holy.

"Honour your father and your mother, so that you may live long in the land the Lord your God is giving you.

"You shall not murder.

"You shall not commit adultery.

"You shall not steal.

"You shall not give false testimony against your neighbour.

"You shall not covet your neighbour's house. You shall not covet your neighbour's wife, or his manservant or maidservant, his ox or donkey, or anything that belongs to your neighbour."

These Ten Commandments are also given in Deuteronomy 5:6–21. As one Christian summarised them, "eight shall not one remember and one honour."

Psalm 23:1–6

King David son of Jesse

"The LORD is my shepherd, I shall lack nothing.

"He makes me lie down in green pastures, he leads me beside quiet waters,

"He restores my soul. He guides me in paths of righteousness for his name's sake.

"Even though I walk through the valley of the shadow of death, I will fear no evil, for you are with me; your rod and your staff, they comfort me.

"You prepare a table before me in the presence of my enemies.

"You anoint my head with oil; my cup overflows.

"Surely goodness and love will follow me all the days of my life, and I will dwell in the house of the Lord forever."

Psalm 108:3–5

King David son of Jesse

"I will praise you, O LORD, among the nations; I will sing of you among the peoples.

"For great is your love, higher than the heavens; your faithfulness reaches to the skies.

"Be exalted, O God, above the heavens, and let your glory be over all the earth."

Isaiah 2:2–4

Isaiah son of Amoz

"In the last days the mountain of the LORD's temple will be established as chief among the mountains; it will be raised above the hills, and all nations will stream to it.

"Many people will come and say, 'Come, let us go up to the mountain of the LORD, to the house of the God of Jacob. He will teach us his ways, so that we may walk in his paths.' The law will go out from Zion, the word of the Lord from Jerusalem.

"He will judge between the nations and will settle disputes for many peoples. They will beat their swords into ploughshares and their spears into pruning hooks. Nation will not take up sword against nation, nor will they train for war anymore."

Isaiah 19:23–25

Isaiah son of Amoz

"In that day there will be a highway from Egypt to Assyria. The Assyrians will go to Egypt and the Egyptians to Assyria. The Egyptians and Assyrians will worship together.

"In that day Israel will be the third, along with Egypt and Assyria, a blessing on the earth.

"The LORD Almighty will bless them, saying, 'Blessed be Egypt my people, Assyria my handiwork, and Israel my inheritance'."

Isaiah 43:1–3

Isaiah son of Amoz

"…Fear not, for I have redeemed you; I have called you by name; you are mine.

"When you pass through the waters, I will be with you; and when you pass through the rivers, they will not sweep over you. When you walk through the fire, you will not be burned; the flames will not set you ablaze.

"For I am the LORD, your God, the Holy One of Israel, your Saviour…"

Isaiah 52:7–10

Isaiah son Amoz

"How beautiful on the mountains are the feet of those who bring good news, who proclaim peace, who bring good tidings, who proclaim salvation, who say to Zion 'Your God reigns!'

"Listen! Your watchmen lift up their voices; together they shout for joy. When the Lord returns to Zion, they will see it with their own eyes.

"Burst into songs of joy together, you ruins of Jerusalem, for the Lord has comforted his people, he has redeemed Jerusalem.

"The LORD will lay bare his holy arm in the sight of all the nations, and all the ends of the earth will see the salvation of our God."

Isaiah 61:1–2

Isaiah son of Amoz
"The Spirit of the Sovereign LORD is on me, because the LORD has anointed me to preach good news to the poor. He has sent me to bind up the broken-hearted,
"to proclaim freedom for the captives and release for the prisoners, to proclaim the year of the LORD's favour and the day of vengeance of our God, to comfort all who mourn."

Micah 4:1–3

Micah of Moresheth
"In the last days the mountain of the LORD's temple will be established as chief among the mountains; it will be raised above the hills, and peoples will stream to it.
"Many nations will come and say, 'Come let us go up to the mountain of the Lord, to the house of the God of Jacob. He will teach us his ways, so that we

may walk in his paths.' The law will go out from Zion, the word of the LORD from Jerusalem.

"He will judge between many peoples and will settle disputes for strong nations far and wide. They will beat their swords into ploughshares and their spears into pruning hooks. Nation will not take up sword against nation, nor will they train for war anymore."

Zechariah 9:9–10

Zechariah son of Berekiah, the son of Iddo
"Rejoice greatly; O daughter of Zion! Shout, Daughter of Jerusalem! See, your king comes to you, righteous and having salvation, gentle and riding on a donkey, on a colt, the foal of a donkey.

"I will take away the chariots from Ephraim and the war-horses from Jerusalem, and the battle bow will be broken. He will proclaim peace to the nations. His rule will extend from sea to sea and from the River to the ends of the earth."

Our Father in Heaven, The Lord's Prayer

Pray anywhere anytime and the Christian prayer is directed to God the Father, in the name of Jesus through the power of the Holy Spirit.

Jesus told his disciples to pray the following prayer and is called the Lord's Prayer. It takes 21 seconds to recite.

Saint Matthew's Gospel 6:9–13:

"…'Our Father in heaven, hallowed be your name,

"your kingdom come, your will be done on earth as it is in heaven.

"Give us today our daily bread.

"Forgive us our debts, as we also have forgiven our debtors.

"And lead us not into temptation, but deliver us from the evil one'."

See also Luke's Gospel 11:2–4

The Great Commission

After the Resurrection, Jesus appeared to the eleven faithful disciples on a Galilee mountain and gave them his 'most dynamic farewell speech of all time, in all of humanity and all of history' and commanded his followers, you and I, to proclaim the Gospel to all the nations (Matthew 28:18–20):

"…All authority in heaven and on earth has been given to me.

"Therefore, go and make disciples of all nations, baptising them in the name of the Father and of the Son and of the Holy Spirit, "and teaching them to obey everything I have commanded you. And surely I will be with you always, to the very end of the age." (Matthew 28:18–20).

See also Matthew 24:14

"And this gospel of the kingdom will be preached in the whole world as a testimony to all nations, and then the end will come." (Matthew 24:14).

Mark 13:10

"And the gospel must first be preached to all nations." (Mark 13:10)

"…Go into all the world and preach the good news to all creation…" (Mark 16:15).

The Eight Beatitudes

The Beatitudes are the Christian Manifesto for the coming Kingdom of God on earth proclaimed by Jesus Christ on his early ministry. They are also described by others as 'Sermon on the Mount', 'Charter of the Kingdom', 'Summary of Christianity', 'The Most Basic Teachings of Our Faith', 'the Proclamation of the Kingdom of God' and 'Christian's identity card'.

Jesus to start his public ministry went to a mountainside and gave this sermon to his disciples:

"Blessed are the poor in spirit, for theirs is the kingdom of heaven.

"Blessed are those who mourn, for they will be comforted.

"Blessed are the meek, for they will inherit the earth.

"Blessed are those who hunger and thirst for righteousness, for they will be filled.

"Blessed are the merciful, for they will be shown mercy.

"Blessed are the pure in heart, for they will see God.

"Blessed are the peacemakers, for they will be called sons of God.

"Blessed are those who are persecuted because of righteousness, for theirs is the kingdom of heaven." (Matthew 5:3–10).

The I Am Statements

The I Am statements are quoted in the Gospel of Saint John, one of Jesus's twelve disciples:

"…I am the bread of life. He who comes to me will never go hungry, and he who believes in me will never be thirsty." (John 6:35).

"…I am the light of the world. Whoever follows me will never walk in darkness, but will have the light of life." (John 8:12).

"…I am the gate for the sheep (door in other versions)…I am the gate; whoever enters through me will be saved…" (John 10:7–9).

"I am the good shepherd. The good shepherd lays down his life for the sheep…I am the good shepherd; I know my sheep and my sheep know me." (John 10:11–14).

"…I am the resurrection and the life. He who believes in me will live, even though he dies; and whoever lives and believes in me will never die…" (John 11:25–26).

"…I am the way and the truth and the life. No-one comes to the Father except through me. If you really knew me, you would know my Father as well…" (John 14:6–7).

"I am the true vine…I am the vine; you are the branches. If a man remains in me and I in him, he will bear much fruit; apart from me you can do nothing." (John 15:1–5).

Jesus's Disciples

In the Gospel of Matthew 10:2–4, Saint Matthew gives the list of the twelve disciples of Jesus who followed him during his public ministry, theoretically one per every tribe of Israel. Earlier Saint Matthew record that brothers Peter and Andrew, both fishermen, were the first disciples, followed by brothers James and John, sons of Zebedee, also their partner fishermen. The fifth was Matthew himself, the tax collector.

From his many disciples, Jesus chose only twelve of them and designated them as Apostles.

1. Simon (Peter)
2. Andrew
3. James son of Zebedee
4. John son of Zebedee
5. Philip
6. Bartholomew (Nathanael in the Gospel of John)
7. Thomas
8. Matthew (Levi in Luke's Gospel)
9. James son of Alphaeus
10. Thaddaeus (Judas son of James in Luke's Gospel; Judas not Iscariot in John's Gospel))
11. Simon the Zealot
12. Judas Iscariot (Judas son of Simon in John's gospel)

Not all the disciples during Jesus's ministry are quoted equally but all are listed.

The Gospel of Mark 3:16–19 also gives the list of the twelve disciples. The Gospel of John lists early four disciples. Acts 1:13 lists the eleven faithful disciples, and in Acts 1:26 Matthias was added to the eleven apostles taking the place of Judas Iscariot.

One has to add one thing that Jesus chose his 'unlettered' disciples and not the other way around.

Examples of Christian Witnessing and Evangelising Saint Paul (Saul of Tarsus) and The Pauline Ministry

Saint Paul (c.2 to 67 AD), an example of a Christian evangelist.

Saint Paul is the greatest missionary, evangelist and theologian in early Christian and church history. A Pharisee in the time of the early Church, he was not among Jesus' twelve disciples but was first mentioned in the Book of Acts for his involvement in the persecution of the early Church, i.e. after Jesus's ascension to heaven and the birth of the church on Pentecost day.

He encountered the Lord Jesus on his journey to Damascus. He preached the Gospel to the Gentiles and wrote 14 books (if Hebrews is included) between the Book of Acts and James of the New Testament, almost half of the New Testament and the greatest was his letter to the Romans. Thus, Paul was transformed from a persecutor of Christ to martyr for Christ.

Saul of Tarsus, as he was known before his conversion, is an apostle of Jesus Christ in the post-Ascension era. In the pre-Ascension era, the Church movement was primarily Jewish but Paul transcended it by conquering the Hellenic world, then to the entire world as we see it today. It is possibly correct to say that Paul founded the Christian Church as a universal church from the early humble start of the 'Nazarenes' or the 'Way' movement.

He founded the first church in Europe, the church in Philippi in Biblical Macedonia, the church that spread westward, then to the New World of Americas in the seventeenth century and later to the South Pacific of Australia and New Zealand.

He was beheaded in Rome under the rule of Emperor Nero and the dates of his birth and martyrdom are disputed. He was a contemporary of Jesus but it is not recorded whether Paul ever saw Jesus in his earthly life.

Saint Maximilian Kolbe

Maximilian Kolbe (1894–1941), an example of a Christian Witness to Christ.

Maximilian Kolbe was a Polish national and priest who grew up between World War I and II and joined the Franciscan Friars. He was arrested by the Gestapo in German-occupied Poland in February 1941 and sent to the infamous Auschwitz concentration camp as prisoner 16770 and in Barrack 14.

When one prisoner had escaped, the guards decided to kill 10 prisoners. One of the ten was a Jewish priest Franciszek Gajowniczek (Francis for short), with a family (wife and four children) to look after and pleaded the guards to save his life.

Maximilian Kolbe volunteered to die instead of Francis the Jewish prisoner because he was not married and had no family of his own to look after. As he was frail and with chronic tuberculosis, the guards agreed.

The ten prisoners were starved for 14 days but four were still alive, Maximilian Kolbe among them. Later they were given a lethal injection of carbonic acid or phenol on 14 August 1941, aged 47.

Father Maximilian Kolbe was canonised and made a saint in 1982 by the Vatican. Francis the Jewish prisoner who survived death through Maximillian Kolbe's sacrifice attended the canonisation and spoke that Father Maximilian Kolbe did not die for one, but he died for you all. Francis lived until his death in 1995 to witness a Christian who gave his life to save others as Christ did for us.

"Greater love has no one than this; that one lay down his life for his friends." (John 15:13).

Billy Graham

Billy Graham (1918–2018), an example of a Christian evangelist.

Reverend Dr William Franklin Graham was born into a Presbyterian Christian family in Charlotte in North Carolina in 1918. It was the environment in his home that brought him in the limelight. At his home, a Bible was set to open in the porch for every goer and comer to see. He said in one of his preaching or writing that when he was a boy, many times he did not want to go to church on Sunday, but he said he was told to go and so he went. He became Christian and was born again in 1934.

That boy became the greatest, the heroic revivalist, evangelist and preacher of the 20th century and perhaps in modern human history – Saint Paul of our time.

William Franklin Graham was ordained in 1939 and married Ruth Bell in 1943. His first crusade was in 1949 in Los Angeles. He started television show in 1951 and began live broadcast from New York in 1957. His last crusade was in June 2005 in New York where about quarter a million people attended.

Billy Graham preached the 'Message of the Cross'. In his preach, he affirmed that Jesus Christ did not die on the cross by accident, but he died by design for our redemption and our salvation. He emphasised once more that Jesus Christ on the Cross took the hand of God in one hand and our hand in another and reconciled them.

He preached the Gospel of Jesus Christ to 7 million in-person while 200 million and more across 185 countries watched his crusades on television or through satellite link-ups. In one day, he preached to 1.1 million in Seoul in 1973 and converted 3.2 million people worldwide. Even his funeral was described as the final crusade.

"With his steely features and piercing blue eyes, he was a powerful figure when he preached in his prime, roaming the stage and hoisting a Bible as he declared Jesus Christ to be the only solution to humanity's problems," one observed. Another rightly quoted that "Billy Graham is one of the world's most beloved evangelist."

He was nicknamed as 'God's ambassador' and 'God's Machine Gun'.

Billy Graham has two sons and three daughters, all evangelists and the Billy Graham Evangelistic Association (BGEA), he set up with his team in the early ministry, is now led by his son Franklin Graham.

His tombstone read 'Preacher of the Gospel of Jesus Christ'.

Faith in Quotations

These quotations help you to understand the Christian faith and are listed in random order:

"If you can show me anytime, anywhere that someone called on Jesus Christ to save them in repentance and faith, and he didn't save them, then I'll close my Bible and never preach again." – Adrian Rogers (1931–2005).

"He's going to turn your Calvary into an Easter and your heartache to a hallelujah." – Adrian Rogers (1931–2005).

"The first time, He stood before Pilate. When He comes again, Pilate will stand before Him." – Adrian Rogers (1931–2005).

"If you took all the references to judgement out of the Bible, you would have little Bible left." – Billy Graham (1918–2018).

"I will not preach easy believism." – Billy Graham (1918–2018).

"Someday you will read or hear that Billy Graham is dead. Don't you believe a word of it? I shall be more alive than I am now. I will just have changed my address. I will have gone into the presence of God." – Billy Graham (1918–2018).

"My home is in heaven. I'm just travelling through this world." – Billy Graham (1918–2018).

"Heaven is where Jesus Christ is, and I'm going to him soon." – Billy Graham (1918–2018).

"If God doesn't punish…, He'll have to apologise to Sodom and Gomorrah." – Ruth Graham (1920–2007).

"George W Bush, the oilman I prayed with to receive Jesus Christ as Saviour and Lord on 3 April 1984 has gone on to become President of the United States of America. All glory to God." – Arthur Blessitt.

"God is not a dancer, he is the dance itself!" – Richard Bohr.

"The modern world…has divorced Christ from His Cross; the Bridegroom and Bride have been pulled apart. What God hath joined together, men have torn asunder…But the Cross without Christ is sacrifice without love." – Fulton J Sheen (1895–1979).

"Unless there is a Good Friday in your life, there can be no Easter Sunday." – Fulton J Sheen (1895–1979).

"The Easter account takes us on a rollercoaster ride following Jesus's journey to the cross, brutal execution and miraculous resurrection. It's a story of man facing death and a world receiving redemption." – Anonymous.

"Christians are being driven out of the Holy Land, leaving it as a kind of Spiritual Disneyland with no local Christians." – Francis.

"The Church lives in Babylon but Babylon does not live within the Church." – Patrick Sookhdeo.

"The more you mow us down, the more we grow. The blood of the martyrs is the seed of the Church." – Tertullian (c.160–225 AD).

"When we pray, we speak to God. When we read the Bible, God speaks to us." – Saint Jerome (347–420 AD).

"Cheap grace is the grace we bestow on ourselves. Cheap grace is the preaching of forgiveness without requiring repentance, baptism without church discipline, communion without confession…cheap grace is grace without discipleship, grace without the cross, grace without Jesus Christ, living and incarnate." – Dietrich Bonhoeffer (1906–1945).

"Christianity is not a teaching, not a philosophy, not even a religion, but it centres on historical events and on historical person of Jesus Christ." – Charles Price.

"It is impossible to rightly govern the world without God and the Bible." – George Washington (1732–1799).

"Not with the Cross of the Saviour behind you, but with your own cross behind the Saviour." – Cyprian Norwid (1821–1883).

"For you I am a bishop, and with you I am a Christian." – Saint Augustine of Hippo (354–430 AD).

"The new is in the old concealed; the old is in the new revealed." – Saint Augustine of Hippo (354–430 AD).

"The Old Testament is the New Testament concealed and the New Testament is the Old Testament revealed." – Anonymous.

"What separate us as believers in Christ is much less than what unites us." – John XXIII (1881–1963).

"When I give food to the poor, they call me a saint. When I ask why they are poor, they call me a communist." – Dom Hélder Câmara (1909–1999).

"(God is love) have no real meaning unless God contains at least two persons." – C S Lewis (1898–1963).

"I see Jesus in every human being. I say to myself, this is hungry Jesus, I must feed him. This is sick Jesus. This one has leprosy or gangrene; I must wash him and tend him. I serve because I love Jesus." – Mother Theresa (1910–1997).

"We are treated as citizens of second class. We prefer to stay here, even crucified sometimes, because in the Gospel it is written that it is given to us not only to believe in Christ but also to suffer for Christ." – Patriarch Bartholomew.

"There is no going to Mount Zion but by the way of Mount Sinai; that is the right straight road." – George Whitefield (1714–1770).

"Secure sinners must hear the thundering of Mount Sinai before we bring them to Mount Zion." – George Whitefield (1714–1770).

"There is always a Ziklag battle before a Zion victory." – Perry Stone.

"I have frequently been threatened with death. I ought to say that, as a Christian, I do not believe in death without resurrection. If they kill me I will rise again…Martyrdom is a grace from God which I do not believe I deserve. But if God accepts the sacrifice of my life, then may my blood be the seed of liberty…A bishop may die, but the Church of God which is the people will never die." – Oscar Romero (1917 –1980).

"Eighty-six years I have served Christ, and He never did me any wrong. How can I blaspheme my King who saved me?" – Saint Polycarp (c.70–155 AD).

"The more completely we focus our attention on our Creator and Lord, the less chance there is of our being distracted by creatures." – Saint Ignatius (c.35–110 AD).

"I consider that the chief dangers which confront the coming century will be religion without the Holy Ghost; Christianity without Christ; forgiveness without repentance; salvation without regeneration; politics without God; and Heaven without Hell." – William Booth (1829–1912).

"I am not waiting for a move of God, I am a move of God!" – William Booth (1829–1912).

"Those born once will die twice and those born twice will die once." – Chuck Missler (1934–2018).

"The crucifixion was not a tragedy, it was a crowning achievement." – Chuck Missler (1934–2018).

"…God does not kill. It is man that wants to do so on God's behalf. To kill in the name of God is blasphemy." – Jorge Mario Bergoglio.

"One has to learn that religion is the manifestation of the most sublime aspects of humanity…Anything else is distortion…" – Abraham Skorka.

"Christianity is the only faith on earth with a virgin womb on one end and an empty tomb at the other." – Rod Parsley.

"Jesus is the most remarkable man who ever lived. He is the centrepiece of our civilisation." – Nicky Gumbel.

"Jesus is the only man who has ever chosen to be born…" – Nicky Gumbel.

"The cost of not becoming a Christian is far greater than the cost of becoming a Christian." – Nicky Gumbel.

"Don't doubt the Creator, because it is inconceivable that accidents alone could be the controller of this universe." – Isaac Newton (1643–1727).

"Jesus walking on earth is more important than man walking on the moon." – James B Irwin (1930–1991).

"…I am a Jew, but I am enthralled by the luminous figure of the Nazarene…" – Albert Einstein (1879–1955).

"I'm convinced more than ever that man finds liberation only when he binds himself to God and commits himself to his fellow man." – Ronald Reagan (1911–2004).

"Though there are times when it may seem like God is silent, he is never absent." – Brian Houston.

"You don't need a telescope, a microscope or a horoscope to realise the fullness of Christ and the emptiness of the universe without him." – The Message Bible.

"The Law condemns the best of us, but Grace saves the worst of us." – Joseph Prince.

"Today we have Christless Christianity and Crossless Christianity." – Joseph Prince.

"The Bible tells us to love our neighbours, and also to love our enemies; probably because they are generally the same people." – G K Chesterton (1874–1936).

"There must be must be a first mover existing above all-and this we call God." – Thomas Aquinas (1225–1274).

"Faith is different from proof; the latter is human, the former is a gift from God." – Blaise Pascal (1623–1662).

"Every unbeliever will die because of his unbelief." (2 Esdras 15:4).

"God did not invent death, and when living creatures die, it gives him no pleasure." (The Wisdom of Solomon 1:13).

"We are to Plunder Hell to Populate Heaven for Calvary's sake." – Reinhard Bonnke.

"I the chief of sinners am, but Jesus died for me." – John Wesley (1703–1791).

"I came, I saw, God conquered." – Charles V (1500–1558) and Jan III Sobieski (1629–1696).

"The Blood of Jesus washes away our past and the Name of Jesus opens up our future." – Jesse Duplantis.

"You will either offend the world and please God, or please the world and offend God." – John Hagee.

"If you are a Christian, your search for approval should be over." – David Jeremiah.

"The Christian church is one of the few organisations in the world that requires a public acknowledgement of sin as a condition for membership." – R C Sproul (1939–2017).

"The Gospel offers forgiveness for the past, new life for the present, and hope for the future." – John Sentamu.

"Only through repentance and faith in Christ can anyone be saved. No religious activity will be sufficient, only true faith in Jesus Christ." – Ravi Zacharias.

"To look up out at this kind of creation and not believe in God is to me impossible." – John Glenn (1921–2016).

"Christianity, if false, is of no importance, and if true, of infinite importance. The only thing it cannot be is moderately important." – C S Lewis (1898–1963).

"Our Christian conviction is that Christ is also the Messiah of Israel. Certainly, it is in the hands of God how and when the unification of Jews and Christians into the people of God will take place." – Benedict XVI.

"This is our land. This is our world. This is our heritage, and with God's help, we shall reclaim this nation for Jesus Christ. And no power on earth can stop us." – D James Kennedy (1930–2007).

"One word from God can change your life." – Chris Oyakhilome.

"God created the world; the laws of nature were created by God. True science tries to find out what God put in the world…" – Pat Robertson.

"The Gospel is the end of religion." – Michael Morrison.

"If you are accused of being a Christian, there should be enough evidence to convict you." – Joyce Meyer.

"Sin's remedy is a sacrifice. This is the message of the whole Bible from beginning to end…all sufficient sacrifice which Jesus made on our behalf on the Cross." – Derek Prince (1915–2003).

"I'm a Christian, a conservative, and a Republican in that order." – Mike Pence.

"President Trump is a Believer and so am I" Mike Pence

"If God does not exist, everything is permitted." – Fyodor M Dostoyevsky (1821–1881).

"Sin is the most expensive thing in the universe. Nothing else can cost so much." – Charles Grandison Finney (1792–1875).

"Mary is arguably the first disciple, someone who lived in the world but also very close to the heart of God." – Anonymous.

"Faith in the resurrection is not a product of the church, but the church herself is born of faith in the resurrection." – Francis.

"The world vitally needs the Gospel of Jesus Christ." – Francis.

"I see the Church as a field hospital after battle." – Francis.

"I will die in bed, my successor will die in prison, his successor will die in the public square." – Francis Eugene George (1937–2015).

"As a Christian, we always fail because we can't become Christ. But I can try at least to emulate the best qualities, even if I may fall short." – Kelsey Grammer.

"…doing what we are called to do, to feed the hungry, clothe the naked, befriend the friendless and love the unlovable." – The Salvation Army's literature.

"I am Cyrus. I am Cyrus." – Harry S Truman (1884–1972).

"Two thousand years ago, a man walked upon the shores of the Sea of Galilee and said the following words 'Follow Me'. Those words changed the course of world history." – Anonymous.

"The Son of God became man in order to heal the separation from God that man's sin had created…Jesus cancelled man's original sin of pride and division and reconciled the world with God…Lord, life is changed not ended…" – Fr. Franco.

"Is the Church changing the world, or the world-changing the church?" – Melody T McCloud.

"Jesus is God clothed in humanity." – K A Schneider.

"Christ is more than a person with a heart…it is the God-Man Christ where spirit meets matter." – Anonymous.

"More than Jews have kept Shabbat. Shabbat has kept the Jews." – Ahad Ha'am (1856–1927).

"Go forth and set the world on fire." Saint Ignatius of Loyola (1491-1556)

"Everybody wants to go to heaven, but nobody wants to die." Anonymous

"The Jewish state has never had a better friend in the White House than your President, Donald J Trump." Donald J Trump

"The most pro-faith president [Donald Trump] in history…he is on the right side of God." Robert Jeffress

"He created me in eternity, before time began, and I will exist for all eternity to come." Sirach 24:9

"He knows all that has ever been and all that ever will be..." Sirach 42:19

"The blood of Christ has the power to atone for an infinite number of sins committed by an infinite number of people throughout the ages, and all whose faith rests in that blood will be saved." Ward Simpson

"All nature honoured him, and for three years he preached the gospel. He wrote no book, he built no church, he had no money, and after 2,000 years, he's the central figure of history, the perpetual theme of all preaching and the pivot around which the events of the world take place." David Jeremiah

"But that year the Saviour of the world was born in that humble place called Bethlehem where deity would invade eternity, and eternity would invade time, and royalty would show up dressed in poverty. Only God could have written such a script." David Jeremiah

"Jesus is the Bible, the walking Bible." Anonymous

"A Christian is another Christ." Anonymous

"If you don't live the Gospel, how can you preach the Gospel?" Anonymous

"We are living in unusual times and navigating uncharted waters! We have a God who is in control and a Saviour who walked on water and calmed the storm. We can intercede for the world, our friends and family and know we have a God who hears and answers prayer." David Wavre

Hymns of Praise

These hymns and Christian songs are selected purely for the purpose of giving the reader the core principles of the Christian faith and teaching and can be found on the internet as lyrics or songs or both. Some are pure Christian literature.

"Commitment of a Christian Martyr"

By an anonymous young man from Rwanda in Africa (source: Dr Robert Morehead/Fellowship of the Unashamed)

I am a part of the fellowship of the Unashamed

I have the Holy Spirit Power the die has been cast

I have stepped over the line the decision has been made

I am a disciple of Jesus Christ.

I won't look back let up slow down back away or be still.

My past is redeemed, my present makes sense, and my future is secure.

I am finished and done with low living, sight walking, small planning, smooth knees, colourless dreams, tame visions, mundane talking, cheap living and dwarfed goals.

I no longer need pre-eminence, prosperity, position, promotions plaudits or popularity.

I don't have to be right first tops recognised praised regarded or rewarded.

I now live by presence, lean by faith, love by patience, lift by prayer and labour by power.

My pace is set, my gait is fast, my goal is Heaven, my road is narrow, my way is rough, my companions few, my Guide is reliable, my mission is clear.

I cannot be bought, compromised, deterred, lured away turned back, diluted or delayed.

I will not flinch in the face of sacrifice hesitate in the presence of adversity, negotiate at the table of the enemy ponder at the pool of popularity or meander in the maze of mediocrity.

I won't give up, back up, let up or shut up until I've preached up, prayed up, paid up, stored up and stayed up for the cause of Christ.

I am a disciple of Jesus Christ.

I must go until He returns give until I drop preach until all know and work until He comes.

And when He comes to get His own

He will have no problem recognising me.

My colours will be clear for "I am not ashamed of the Gospel because it is the power of God for the salvation of everyone who believes." (Romans 1:16).

"When I Say, 'I Am a Christian'"

Carol Wimmer 1988
When I say, "I am a Christian,"
I'm not shouting, "I've been saved!"
I'm whispering, "I feel lost sometimes!"
That's why I chose this way
When I say, "I am a Christian,"
I don't speak with human pride
I'm confessing that I stumble needing God to be my guide
When I say, "I am a Christian,"
I'm not trying to be strong
I'm professing that I'm weak and pray for strength to carry on
When I say, "I am a Christian,"
I'm not bragging of success
I'm admitting that I've failed and cannot even pay the debt
When I say, "I am a Christian,"
I don't think I know it all!
I submit to my confusion asking humbly to be taught
When I say, "I am a Christian,"
I'm not claiming to be perfect

My flaws are all too visible but God believes I'm worth it
When I say, "I am a Christian,"
I still feel the sting of pain
I have my share of heartache,
that's why I seek God's name
When I say, "I am a Christian,"
I do not wish to judge
I have no authority…
I only know I'm loved

"Noon Ed Dimma" (N of the Blood)

Assyrian Lyrics by Vian (taken from the Internet) and translated into English by the author.

It represents the suffering and persecution of the Christians of the Middle East by the followers of the main religion. N which stands for Nazarene, is a derogatory word to mean Christian, was marked in red on the forefront of every Christian property for the purpose of hate and confiscation.

N adorned in the colour of blood was marked on our houses we are slaughtered in our motherland they destroyed our antiquities and our churches
What to do?
Where to go?
What is next?
With our own eyes, we see.

Either we deny our identity and shalmakh* or to the rule of the beast we harken

Either we turn before the sword and kneel or we carry our load and depart

We will not deny our Christianity in Nineveh, our history will not be obliterated, we will not accept the end of our heritage, they will not take away our nation

Come, my brother, you and I in the love of Christ, the compassionate hand in hand we pull together and rescue ourselves from this tragedy

O Nazarene for the sake of thy Name, the sacrifice of thy Virgin Mother, you taught us stillness and peace for love thy Blood was shed

We lift thy Name in prayers with broken heart and supplications, let thy Mercy rain down and save the city of the cities

* shalmakh is Assyrian word for converting to the main religion of the Middle East.

Christian Dictionary

These definitions are arranged in random order.

Holy Bible (Holy Book) = is the written Word of God or 'autobiography from God' revealed to humans to follow and obey. It starts from the book of Genesis (the creation and the beginning of man) and ends with the book of Revelation (the vision about the second coming of Jesus Christ and the end of the age.

The Bible in all is about Jesus Christ, prophesied in the Old Testament through the nation of Israel and fulfilled in the New Testament.

The Bible starts with the verse "In the beginning God created the heavens and the earth" and ends with the verse "The grace of the Lord Jesus be with God's people. Amen." The Bible means book and is one book and derives its name from the Greek Biblion.

Old Testament = is the Hebrew books of the Bible from Genesis to Malachi. These books are about God, the creation, the flood and the nation of Israel and the Law of Moses written before the birth of Jesus Christ but Christ is prophesied. Old Testament is derived from the old covenant, the Mosaic covenant on Mount Sinai.

Pentateuch = or the Torah is the first five books of the Old Testament from Genesis to Deuteronomy, possibly written by Moses.

Tanakh = is a Hebrew Bible or the Old Testament (Torah, Prophets and Psalms). Jesus read this Bible while on earth.

Septuagint = (from Septuaginta in Latin for 70) is the first translation of the Hebrew Bible (Old Testament) into the Greek language in the third and second century BC in Alexandria.

New Testament = is the Greek books of the Bible from Saint Matthew's Gospel to Revelation. It is about

God and his Son Jesus, the revealed Christ and his Gospel. These books document Jesus Christ's mission on earth and were written years after the Resurrection of Jesus Christ. The central theme of these books is Grace through faith. New Testament is derived from the new covenant, Jesus's atoning sacrifice on Calvary.

Apocrypha = (from Greek) or Deuterocanonical books or Intertestamental books are the books of the Bible between the Old Testament and the New Testament but most modern versions of the Bibles omit them.

Deuterocanonical Books were part of the Septuagint Greek text but the 'Hebrew Canon was truncated to 39 books' but are still canonical in the Catholic Church for example.

Gospel = Evangelium in Latin and Evangelio in Greek is one of the first four books commencing the New Testament written by a Gospel writer, Gospel of Matthew(disciple), Gospel of Mark (not a disciple), Gospel of Luke (not a disciple) and Gospel of John (disciple). The first three Gospels are called the Synoptic Gospels. Simply, the Gospel is the Good News (Luke 2:10) of Jesus Christ, his birth, atoning death, resurrection and his saving grace for his church.

It is abbreviated in a simple statement 'four ministries, one Jesus' or 'four Gospels but one Gospeller'.

Holy Scripture = texts written by men inspired by God through the Holy Spirit; the contents of the whole Bible.

God = 'is uncreated, self-existent, infinite, sovereign, eternal. These attributes are His alone'. The origin of the word God is gothic. God is the first person of the Holy Trinity.

Jesus Christ = is Jesus 'The Christ' that was 'concealed' in the Old Testament but now 'revealed' in the New Testament, which means Jesus the Anointed or Jesus the Messiah is Jesus the Evangelist.

Jesus Christ is the Greek name Iesous Christos for the Hebraic name Yeshua Ha-Mashiach and Yeshua Mshiho in Aramaic (Syriac). Jesus means God saves (Matthew 1:21) and Christ means anointed. Immanuel, in Hebrew, means God is with us, is a title. Jesus is the second person of the Holy Trinity.

Holy Spirit = is the third person of the Holy Trinity. He empowered the Virgin Mary to be with child. He was the dove above Jesus in his baptism and the Paraclete on Pentecost day. The Holy Spirit communicates us with the Father and the Son.

Virgin Mary = Maria in Greek and Miriam in Hebrew and Aramaic is the Mother of Jesus according to the New Testament. Isaiah 7:14 prophecies Jesus's mother and His birth: "…The virgin will be with child and will give birth to a son, and will call him Immanuel." Virgin Mary was part of Jesus's ministry.

Old covenant = is God's covenant with Moses on Mount Sinai – the Ten Commandments.

New covenant = is Jesus's sacrifice on the Cross of Mount Calvary.

Law and Grace = Law is the Ten Commandments given by God to Moses (do that or don't do that). Grace is the fruit (free gift) of Jesus's sacrifice on the cross (without do that or don't do that). Law cannot save, but Grace saves. Law, for example, says 'stone her', but grace says 'go and sin no more'.

The Flood of Noah = the global flood that eliminated the contaminated human race and only eight faithful people were saved in the floatable ark

Epistle = or Letter is any letter of the New Testament.

Canon Law = the way the church organises itself in sets of rules, regulations and guidelines.

Apocalypse = from Greek Apokalupsis is the book of Revelation, the last book of the Bible. It is the vision of Saint John, the last surviving disciple of Jesus Christ about the end of the Age and the second coming of Jesus Christ.

Church = Ekklesia or Iglesia in Greek is the whole community of the baptised or the 'called out' of the world and represents the union of believers in Jesus Christ (his body). The first church was birthed on Pentecost day in the upper room in Jerusalem, 50 days after the Resurrection. The church (bride of Christ) is a Hebraic version of the Assembly or the Knesset.

Gnostic Gospels = are the thirteen 'pseudo-Christian' books unknown until 1945. The Gnostics, Jewish sect at the time of Jesus assert that knowing God comes through 'knowledge' and shun the evil world.

Biblical Parable = or 'picture language' is an illustration of Christian belief in a simple story narrative, for example, the story of the Samaritan man or the Prodigal son.

Ascension of Jesus Christ = forty days after the Resurrection, Jesus was taken into heaven in the presence of his eleven faithful disciples. Simply, Jesus's return to the Father after His mission on earth was complete.

Pentecost = (in Greek) or Shavuot (in Hebrew) symbolises the birth of the church by the indwelling power of the Holy Spirit sent from Heaven 50 days after the Resurrection of Jesus Christ. On Pentecost Day begins the nucleus parish of the early Church, the first church service and Jesus hands on the ministry to the Church. Pentecost Sunday is also called Whitsunday.

Church age = or Grace age is the period from Pentecost until the Rapture of Christians that will usher the Tribulation. Another belief is from Pentecost to Jesus's second coming.

Baptism = (from Baptismos in Greek) or Water Baptism (Christening) is water baptism symbolising the death of Jesus Christ (under water) and his resurrection (above water) and it replaces infant circumcision of the

Old Testament. Baptism is officiated in the name of the Father, the Son and the Holy Spirit. Water baptism also symbolises washing away our sins (death of old self) and (rebirth of a new self in Christ). For infants, it removes the original sin from the soul but for adults, water baptism is preceded by 'repentance'.

Baptism of the Holy Spirit = is spiritual baptism officiates by the Holy Spirit (the third person in the Trinity) like on the Day of Pentecost. Baptism of the Holy Spirit is the second baptism after water baptism.

Confirmation = or baptismal renewal is a sacrament after baptism meant for 'strengthening and perfecting' the baptised.

Holy Trinity = or Triune God, is that God the Father, Jesus the Son and the Holy Spirit are one. The word Trinity is not in the Bible but means three persons united in one God.

It is more exemplified in the eastern Sign of the Cross: "In the name of the Father, the Son and the Holy Spirit, one God, amen."

Sin and repentance = sin is the rejection of God's authority by breaking God's law or commandments or a separation wall that keeps man away from God. ("All wrong-doing is sin" (1 John 5:17) and "sin is lawlessness" (1 John 3:4)). Sin was first created by Satan when he rebelled against God.

Repentance is turning away from sin to a changed life and a changed mind to the mind of God-returning to God.

Original sin = or the first sin is the sin inherited by us from the lineage of Adam for his disobedience to God's command.

Prayer = is a conversation or communication with God, you talk and God listens. In reading the Bible, God talks and you listen.

Bible versions = different translations from original scriptures which are written either in Hebrew or Greek or Aramaic (Syriac).

Denominations = the Christian Church based in Rome split in 1054 AD between Roman Catholic Church (Latin Church) and Byzantium Church (Greek Church or Orthodox Church) based in Constantinople. The remaining Roman Church split in 1517 AD into Rome based Latin Church and the Reformation Churches (sometimes politically labelled Protestant churches).

The Vulgate Bible = the Latin translation of the Holy Bible completed by St. Jerome in the fourth century. It was in general use until the modern translations that followed the Reformation.

King James Version = was published in 1611 in Jacobean English at the time of King James I who oversaw the editing and printing of the Holy Bible. In 2011, the church celebrated 400 years of its publication.

Canonical Gospels = the four Gospels which form the canon which is the basic teaching and belief of the Christian church. Other gospels (if existed) are un-canonical.

The Promised Land = is the land subtended between the Nile River and the Euphrates River that God has promised to give to the Israelites through Abraham, Isaac, Jacob and the 12 tribes.

Israel = or Israelites are the descendants of Jacob (son of Isaac son of Abraham) recorded in Genesis through his twelve sons, later identified as the twelve tribes of Israel. Exiled and oppressed in Egypt they returned to their ancestral homeland or the Promised Land given to them by God. Other names may refer to Israel like Hebrews or Jews.

Jews = single Jew, was coined after the Israelites went into exile. It has become a national-cum-religious identity.

King David = son of Jesse from the tribe of Judah and the second King of Israel after King Saul. He is the father of King Solomon who built the first temple of God. King David conquered Zion and Jerusalem and is attributed to be the founder of the Jewish nation.

Jewish Festivals = or Feasts of the Lord are seven (apart from the Sabbaths) commanded by God to Moses for Israel to celebrate as recorded in Leviticus 23. These are the Feast of Passover, the Feast of Unleavened Bread, the Feast of First-fruits, the Feast of Weeks

(Pentecost), the Feast of Trumpets, the Day of Atonement and the Feast of Tabernacles.

Hanukkah = or the Feast of Dedication or Feast of Lights is Intertestamental event (Book of 2 Maccabees) to celebrate the re-dedication of the Second Temple to God after being desecrated by the Gentiles. Hanukkah is represented by eight-branched candelabrum.

Purim = is a Jewish feast to celebrate the survival of the Jews from a plot to eradicate them during Esther's time as Queen (Book of Esther).

Pharisees, Sadducees and Scribes = Jewish sects or groups at the time of the New Testament. The first two dealt with the Holy Scriptures and their interpretation while the Scribes involved with writing and copying of the Holy Scriptures.

Kingdom of God and Kingdom of Heaven = may refer to one thing. A kingdom that is ruled by Jesus Christ the moment when we accept and confess faith in Jesus Christ filled with love, joy and peace.

The Millennium Reign = is also the Kingdom of God or the Kingdom of Heaven that will begin with Jesus's second coming. It is a heavenly kingdom on earth ruled by King Jesus Christ for a millennium.

The Temple = the First Temple is the temple built by King Solomon son of David in Jerusalem about 950 BC on Mount Mariah that was destroyed by Nebuchadnezzar king of Babylon when he seized

Jerusalem in 586 BC. It was a place of worship and animal sacrifice.

The Second Temple is the temple that was rebuilt by the order of Cyrus, King of Persia and expanded by King Herod but smaller than the First Temple. This temple was attended by Jesus and it was destroyed in 70 AD by the Roman army. What you see now is the Western Wall or the Wailing Wall of that destroyed temple.

The Third Temple is yet to be built and preparations are underway following the unification of Jerusalem in 1967. Building the third temple in Jerusalem in Israel is pre-requisite for Christ's return.

Times of the Gentiles = the time when the Jews no longer rule themselves but ruled by the Gentiles. This period has lasted from the fall of Jerusalem in 586 BC to 1948 when the modern State of Israel was re-created, then followed by the liberation of other Biblical lands in 1967.

Jews and Gentiles = Jews are descendants of Abraham through Isaac, Jacob and the twelve sons. Gentiles are outside that lineage like the Greeks and Romans, for example. In Biblical times they were delineated as the people of circumcision and people of un-circumcision.

Circumcision = is a traditional practise but not faith-related involving surgical removal of the foreskin in male babies. Some babies are born circumcised.

Abomination of the desolation = idols in the Holy place

Shalom = shalom in Hebrew or shlomo in Aramaic (Syriac) is peace and wholeness and complete-time in God's presence.

Holocaust = is a Biblical word and means burnt offerings to God. It is secularly used to describe the extermination of the Jews during WWII which the Jews call Shoah.

The suffering church = or the persecuted church is suffering by Christians or churches for confessing faith in Jesus Christ.

Jerusalem = the undivided and eternal city of the Jewish people where heaven and earth meet and where Jesus meets humanity. Currently, it is the capital of the State of Israel. Jerusalem is also described by Christian scholars as the 'Spiritual Capital of the World'.

Nineveh = one of the capitals of the Assyrian Empire located on the banks of River Tigris. The Assyrians are highly recorded in the Old Testament as the major power until the fall of Nineveh in 612 BC at the hands of the Babylonians and the Medes. Now all are Assyrians are Christian in various denominations.

Chalcedon = Jesus has two natures, fully human and fully divine. Non-Chalcedon, Jesus has one nature, divine only following the Council of Chalcedon in 451 AD.

Prophet = a man or woman sent by God to lead, direct and correct His people.

Prophecy = Biblical prophecy is the power and sovereignty of God for revealing the future from the beginning or declaring end time from the beginning or 'God's blueprint for the future'. Simply, it is history written in advance on the basis of prediction and fulfilment, for example, Isaiah prophesied Jesus's birth and Daniel prophesied Jesus's entry into Jerusalem.

Lent = (from Latin word Lenten for spring) is a fasting season for forty days (excluding Sundays) that starts from Ash Wednesday and concludes with the Resurrection of the Lord Jesus Christ. It is a preparation for Easter through fasting, penance, giving and prayer. It mirrors Jesus's fasting for forty days and forty years of Israel in the wilderness.

Holy Week = or the Passion Week or 'the week that changed the world' or 'a week above all weeks' is the week that precedes Easter. It starts with Palm Sunday in remembrance of Jesus's triumphal entry into Jerusalem, then the Last Supper on Thursday (Gethsemane), the Crucifixion on Friday (Golgotha), then the Holy Saturday (Stillness).

The Dead Sea Scrolls = the first scrolls were discovered by a Bedouin shepherd in 1947 in Khirbet Qumran on the West Bank. The Dead Sea is now in Israel and the discovery of more scrolls lasted until 1956. They contained manuscripts dating back to the time of

Jesus, and the Book of Isaiah of the Old Testament is written on copper, not leather.

The manuscripts were hidden in sealed clay jars possibly taken out of Jerusalem to be protected from the Romans.

The seven churches = are the seven churches in west Asia Minor that appear in the Book of Revelation (chapters 2 and 3). Jesus Christ's testimony through apostle John to each church. These churches were chosen as seven examples that would apply for other unnamed churches. The churches were Ephesus, Smyrna, Pergamum, Thyatira, Sardis, Philadelphia and Laodecia.

Eschatology = or end times prophecies (from Greek Eschatos meaning last). These are Biblical events at end times or when the church age ends that will include the Rapture, Tribulations, Battle of Armageddon, Millennium Reign and the final judgement.

End of the age = we are in Church age but when Jesus return, the Church's age will end and Jesus will begin the Millennium Reign or age for a millennium while Satan is bound.

Sabbath = is the seventh day of the week and is a day of rest and worship. It replicates the six days of creation and the seventh day as the day of rest. Sabbath is a Hebraic term and it begins from Friday sunset to Saturday sunset ("there was evening and there was morning"). Later the early church adopted Sunday as the day of rest instead of Saturday.

Christmas and Easter = Christmas or Feast of the Nativity or Birthday of Jesus Christ celebrated on 25 December in the modern calendar. Orthodox Churches follow the old calendar (it falls on 7 January). The name originates from 'Christ Mass' or 'Christ Service' long before the Reformation.

Easter or Easter Sunday is the Resurrection Day and the 'empty tomb' to mark Jesus rising from the tomb and conquering death. It falls on the first Sunday (after the full moon after 21 March) for both calendars.

Advent = is a time or season of reflection, prayer and preparing in minds and hearts, the Birth of our Lord Jesus Christ at Christmas or his second coming. Traditionally, Advent season starts four weeks before Christmas and lasts until Christmas Day. Advent means 'arrival', 'the arrival of Jesus Christ into the world'.

Epiphany = the manifestation of the divinity of Jesus Christ to the world-nations and peoples, represented in the three Magi who welcomed God in Jesus Christ.

Lamb of God = is Jesus Christ on the cross substituting the Jewish Passover's sacrificial lamb.

Son of God = born of God. Jesus Christ is the Son of God.

Son of man = is the son of Adam in Hebrew, is a Messianic title in the Old Testament.

Hosanna = is Greek for ('save us please') in Hebrew. Hoshiana.

Hallelujah = or Alleluia is originally Aramaic means praise Jehovah or praise the Lord in Hebrew.

Jehovah = or Yahwe is the name of God or Mighty One. Adonai is the Lord and Elohim is the title of God.

I am who I am = or 'I AM' means God.

Nephilim = a hybrid between fallen angels (sons of God) and daughters of men that occurred before the Flood of Noah.

Miracle = is the power of God that transcends the physical laws of nature, for example turning water into wine, walking on water and feeding the five thousand on two fish and five loaves. A miracle is also defined as supernatural.

Paradise = is a stage before heaven.

Heaven = is God's throne, the presence of God and place of righteousness for all believers in Jesus Christ.

Hades = Hades (Greek) or Infernus in Latin or Sheol in Hebrew is an interim abode for the saved and unsaved departed souls.

Hell = Hell (English) for Gehenna or Valley of Hinnom. It defines the absence of God and place of torment for the fallen and non-believers in Jesus Christ after the day of judgement.

Purgatory = the word Purgatory is not in the Bible and is not emphasised by all the churches. Purgatory is a place for the soul to be purified before reaching heaven when the soul is in a state of grace but requires mercy of God for admission into heaven.

Holy Communion = or Eucharist or Thanksgiving or Corpus Christi is the body and blood of Jesus Christ symbolised in bread and wine 'in remembrance' of him – an encore of the Last Supper. The bread symbolises his broken body and the wine his blood that was shed for the forgiveness of sin(s).

Eternity = timeless state after death either eternal salvation in the presence of God or eternal damnation in the absence of God.

Apostasy = defection or falling away from the true faith.

Heresy = or heretic is accepting what is contrary to Biblical beliefs.

Blasphemy = from Greek is lack of reverence to everything sacred.

Conversion = is 'spiritual encounter with God' that transforms from one unviable form to another viable form.

Confession = or Reconciliation is a reconciliation of man with God.

Testimony = is the journey and the power of God that leads to the truth of Jesus Christ.

Evangelism = is to preach or take the Gospel to unreached or unconverted people and making them disciples.

Witnessing = is to witness or testify or share what you have 'seen and heard' on matters of faith.

Sacraments = or Mysteries are two sacraments in the church, Baptism first and Holy Communion second. Baptism may be combined with confirmation and Holy Communion with Confession in some churches. This may differ from denomination to denomination. Sacraments were instituted by Jesus Christ and imply Grace.

Christianity = faith in Jesus Christ and believing his Gospel.

Priest = or Kohen in Hebrew is the one who offers sacrifices to God on behalf of man-animal sacrifices in the Hebrew Bible or spiritual sacrifice in the church.

Deacon = is derived from Greek and is equivalent to Hebrew word Shamash or servant who serve in a church.

John the Baptist = or John the Baptiser is the last prophet and preacher of the Old Testament although he is only mentioned in the New Testament. He is a relative of Jesus through Mary his mother. He preached water baptism in the River Jordan for the remission of sin and as a forerunner for Jesus public ministry.

Apostolic = means in line with the first apostles or disciples of Jesus Christ who received the Holy Spirit on Pentecost Sunday.

Rapture of the Church = (Harpazo in Greek) is when the dead in Christ rise first, then the living will be caught up (and be changed) with Jesus in the air before the tribulation. Biblical scholars mostly advocate this point, not mid or post-tribulation. The word Rapture is not in the Bible but is inherent in Saint Paul's letters.

Antichrist = end times prophecy; antichrist or pseudo-Christ is the one who takes the place of Christ. A man in the personification of Satan (Satan incarnate) to distract the world from Jesus Christ and his church and his number is 666. Antichrist is "the man who denies that Jesus is the Christ" (1 John 2:22) and "who do not acknowledge Jesus Christ" (2 John 1:7)

Mark of the beast = end times prophecy; is a mark on the right hand or on the forehead. This mark is the name of the beast or the number of his name and the number is 666 (Book of Revelation). This mark is associated with followers of antichrist.

Tribulation = a total of seven years wrath divided in half; 3.5 years each with the mid being, the mid-tribulation. The last 3.5 years (Great Tribulation) being more severe in suffering and that will end with the battle of Armageddon and the second return of Jesus Christ. This is the end times prophecy.

The battle of Armageddon = the evil spirit of the world (led by Satan and the antichrist) will make war against the Lamb (Jesus Christ) and the believers. The battle in the Valley of Megiddo which is north of Israel will end with the victory of the Lamb (Revelation 16 & 17). This is end times prophecy that will occur after the

Tribulation. Armageddon is from Har Megiddo or Mount Megiddo in Hebrew.

Gog and Magog = Gog leads Magog from the north (nations of Satan) to march against God's people (Revelation and Ezekiel 38 and 39).

Parousia = is Greek for the second coming (return) of Jesus Christ at the end of the tribulation.

Christian marriage = Christian marriage is a union between a man and a woman, both baptised and lifelong for the purpose of creating a healthy family in a healthy society. Christian marriage is also termed as a 'divine institution'.

Born again = a Christian is born twice, once in physical birth and the second in spiritual birth that is from God above.

Ark of the Covenant = is a replica of the Temple of God on earth, as it is in heaven.

Menorah = a six-branched candelabrum used in the sanctuary by Moses and later in the Temple in Jerusalem. It represents the six days of creation.

Tithe = or Tithing is to give to God 10% of your income or produce according to Old Testament practise.

The Word = is Jesus Christ before the incarnation or Jesus Christ before Christmas.

Logos = the written word of God.

Rhema = the spoken word of God.

One-verse theology = is to base one's faith on a single Bible verse rather than the whole Bible.

Gap theory = is a belief by some Christians or non-Christians that there is a time gap or discontinuity between Genesis verse 1:1 and 1:2 or that these first two verses of the Bible are misplaced. This idea surfaced only in the nineteenth century.

Replacement theology = is a belief by some Christians, but not by all, that God has finished with Jewish people as the chosen people for rejecting Christ, and that the Church or Christianity has replaced them; no longer Israel and Jerusalem but the Church and Heaven. The shift of the centre of Christianity from Jerusalem to Antioch, Alexandria and Rome ended the dominance of the Messianic Judaism, bringing in Romanised and Hellenised Church.

Opposition to this theology argues that Christianity does not replace Judaism but is a continuation.

Fulfilment theology = is a softer version of Replacement theology in that the Old Testament being fulfilled by the coming of Jesus Christ and the birth of the church.

Dominion theology = the belief by some Christians that the church should have dominion on the rest of the society according to Genesis when God granted man dominion over the earth.

Liberation theology = is the mixing of Christian faith and social justice and in somewhat mixing Christianity with materialism to elevate the poor and the oppressed. It found roots in oppressed and poor Latin America.

The Day-Age theory = is a belief by some that the days of creation in Genesis 1 are not literal 24-hour days but times or periods.

Christian Zionists = the belief by some Christians, that the creation of the modern State of Israel in 1948 is the fulfilment of the Biblical prophecy prior to Jesus's second coming. All Christian Zionists are Christian but not all Christians are Christian Zionists.

Christian apology = a Christian apologist is one who stands for the defence of Christianity and Christian beliefs.

Worship = the service of praise and honour to the worthy God.

Saint = is a person wholly committed to God, who is on fire with the love of God

Messianic Jews = Jews who believe in Jesus as the Messiah or the Christ. Messianic but keep their Jewish culture and tradition. Messianic Jews made inroads after the 1967 six-day war between Israel and its hostile neighbours with re-conquering of Judea and Samaria and the reunification of Jerusalem. They are Jews with a blend of Evangelical Christianity and they mirror as they think that the first disciples were Messianic Jews or Jewish evangelists.

Zionism = derived from Mount Zion in Jerusalem is different from Judaism. Judaism is the Jewish faith, but Zionism is Jewish nationalism that advocates that the Holy Land or 'Eretz Yisrael' is the national home for the

Jewish people. Anti-Zionism and the 'Evangelical Left' oppose that.

The Samaritans = from Samaria, the land between Galilee and Judea. Samaritans are either partially Israelites in origin or not but profess or adopt Judaism; currently are a small ethnoreligious group of under 1,000 people and live either in Israel proper or east of Jordan River. They believe in the five books of Moses only that are written in original Aramaic, not in Hebrew. Of course, they deny Jesus.

House church = unregistered or underground churches following the pattern of the early church which was based on house churches until the third century. In present times, house churches grow in countries where Christians are persecuted or forbidden to practise their faith like the church in China for example.

Satan = is the fallen archangel Lucifer described as an angel of the Abyss, father of lies, the dragon, the accuser and the destroyer. Satan in Hebrew meaning the adversary and devil in Greek meaning the slanderer ("…who leads the whole world astray…" as in Revelation 12:9). Demons are lower versions.

Son of perdition = follower of Satan or the antichrist.

The Catholic Church = or the universal church or the Latin Church is apostolic church presided by the Pope in succession to the first Pope and Bishop of Rome. Saint Peter and its ecclesiastical high structure are based in the Vatican in Rome. It differs from other churches by many traditions added along the line from the early church and Virgin Mary, mother of Jesus, is revered as an intercessor.

The Orthodox Church = is the Greek Church that split from the Catholic Church in 1054 AD at the time of Pope Leo IX and Patriarch Michael and is presided by the Patriarch in Saint Andrew's Cathedral in Constantinople. In 1965, Pope Paul VI and Patriarch Athenagoras reconciled the two churches.

The Protestant Reformation = is the reformed church that is rooted in the Reformation that was triggered by theologian Martin Luther.

Martin Luther (1483–1546) was a Catholic monk and theologian who on 31 October 1517 'nailed' his ninety-five theses to the door of Wittenberg Castle church in Germany in opposition to the Catholic Church and its teaching. He was excommunicated by Pope Leo X on 3 January 1521, and in the year 1533 marked the start of Luther's movement in Germany and later worldwide. This movement triggered the Reformation movement in the Western church and the split from the main Catholic Church centred in Rome. The reformed church is an offshoot of the Catholic Church and a church that is neither Catholic nor Orthodox is a Reformed church exemplified in the Evangelicals. Their emphasis is on scripture alone, without any tradition added, unlike both the Catholic and Orthodox churches.

Protestantism is a secular term rather than a religious term for those who were Catholics but opted for a Reformed church that is associated with Martin Luther and John Calvin teachings. Christians, a critic of the Reformation preferred reforming the church within rather than splitting the church and the rollercoaster that followed.

The Coptic Church = established in Egypt in 47 AD by Saint Mark (under Nero) the writer of the second Gospel. It is an ethnic Egyptian church, descendants of Biblical Egypt of ancient times. It splits from main Christianity in the fifth century over issues of human and divine nature of Christ. They believe in the single divine nature of Christ, not in the two-nature, the main Christianity believers.

The Vatican = is the seat of the head of the Roman Catholic Church presided by the Pope or Bishop of Rome and the hierarchy of the church.

The Vatican gained recognition from the Italian government in 1929, and politically is a member of the General Assembly at the United Nations but has no seat on the Security Council.

The Crusades = or Crusaders were Christian volunteers from Europe who responded to calls for arms to help Eastern Christians in Asia Minor and to reverse the invasion of the Holy Land. It started in 1096 and lasted until about 1270 in eight major campaigns.

Pope Urban II and the Church approved the mobilisation in 1095 in a speech by the Pope in Clemont in France on 27 November of that year. The cause or motive of the Crusade was right, but mistakes may have occurred during the latter campaigns and the term Crusade is modern and derogatory.

Inquisition = like the Roman Inquisition or the Spanish Inquisition occurred in Catholic nations like the Romans and the Spanish. Its purpose was to suppress heresy and protect the Christian faith and for the heretics to defend themselves and to prove that they are innocent or guilty and to repent when found guilty. The trials were civil and the church was not involved.

Flavius Josephus = Jewish writer and historian who lived in Jerusalem (under the Romans) from 37 to 100 AD and documented Jesus's trial.

Hermeneutic and Exegesis = hermeneutic sets the rules and methods for interpretation. Exegesis applies those methods and rules to explain a Biblical text.

***

John 1:1 = "In the beginning was the Word, and the Word was with God, and the Word was God." The 'Word' is Logos in Greek which means Jesus.

John 3:3 = "In reply Jesus declared, 'I tell you the truth, unless a man is born again, he cannot see the

Kingdom of God'." This verse is widely used by the Reformed church.

John 3:16 = "For God so loved the world that he gave his one and only Son, that whoever believes in him shall not perish but have eternal life." This one verse summarises the whole Bible and is widely used by the Reformed church.

***

Sanctified = means set apart to God (or holiness). Sanctification is a process to become righteous with God. Sanctification leads to justification.

Justified = exalted to the spiritual level to meet God's standards through faith in Jesus Christ and by his shed blood on the cross.

Glorified = higher form of sanctification.

Redemption = or redeemed means no longer enslaved to sin but freed by the Redeemer, Jesus Christ, who paid the ransom for your freedom, sin removed and you are restored to the original place.

Atonement = the forgiveness of sin paid by Jesus on the cross.

Penance = the undoing of sin by repentance and other selfless means.

Grace = God's empowerment or free gifts from God, that is unearned, undeserved and unmerited.

Love and charity = love (or Agape in Greek) is charity and charity is love. Love is God's love for humanity and in return of humanity's love for God. Christian love is agape love among Christians.

Mercy and Justice = mercy is God's compassion. Justice is God's justice based on truth and righteousness. Mercy is more powerful than justice.

Righteousness = right with God and life not touched by sin.

Forgiveness = the past is obliterated (sin is forgiven) the future is granted…

Charismatic = from Charis (Greek for Grace) is the spontaneous manifestation of the Holy Spirit in the life of believer or believers (church) with gifts of power, healings and miracles and the outcome is spiritual renewal and hearts set on fire for God.

Mystery = the once unknown has become known through God's revelation. For example, the gospel that was sent to the Jews spread to the Gentiles.

Hope and Faith = hope is faith in the unseen future as in the resurrection of the dead. Faith is fulfilled hope. Faith and hope go together.

Anointing = Power of God through man.

Free will and Predestination=Christianity teach that man was given a free will. Predestination is not taught but God is capable of doing that.

Grace and Hyper-Grace = grace is defined above but hyper-grace means a believer's future sins are automatically omitted by the hyper-grace of God-but this is not a Christian doctrine.

Speaking in tongues = is speaking to God in spirit not mind. It is empowerment by the Holy Spirit to speak in another language without prior knowledge (Acts 2:4). Speaking in tongues is also called 'baptism of the Holy Spirit'.

Revival = is a Christian awakening or Christian renewal of the Christian faith in the life of the church. Revival is a move of God in the life of Christians or the church and set people ablaze and the explosion of the church. Revival is a transition from stagnant church, distant from the Holy Spirit to live church filled with the outpouring of the Holy Spirit.

Prophesying = is peaking to men (church).

Excommunication = is the authority of the church to deprive the right of church membership.

Body, soul and spirit = spirit impacts the soul which in turn impact the body; here the soul is the link

The body is the biological senses and the soul is the consciousness (mind/will/emotion) and the spirit is the fruit of the latter. Good spirit pleases God and is multiplied but the bad spirit is away from God and is doomed.

Death = physical or biological death (the first death) is defined as a separation of the body from soul and spirit.

Spiritual death at Judgement (second death) is a separation of the soul from God and is eternal. Saved souls, is eternity with God and unsaved souls, is an eternity without God

***

Religion = religion generally is a 'system of beliefs'. Religion is mostly outwards and relates man and creation (nature) and deity (if included). Christianity is a faith inside-is living in the Kingdom of God. The secular term of 'organised religion' refers to any religion that is institutionalised, compared to minor religion which has no structure.

Proselytising = from Greek is attempting to convert people or person by human efforts. Unlike evangelism which is based on preaching the message and the free will for conversion.

Theism and atheism = theism is a belief in God. An atheist is the one who does not believe in the existence of God.

Pantheism = is the belief in all gods and the universe as a product of god(s).

Creationist and evolutionist = creationist from creation is the one who believes that God created the universe and life (young earth in Genesis 1:1) as opposed to evolutionist from evolution the one who thinks that the universe and life evolved over a period of billions of years. The latter is also known as Neo-Darwinism

Historical Jesus = is not Jesus Christ as recorded in the Bible but Jesus as a man according to secular opinions or critics.

Idolatry = worshipping the created rather than the creator, or substituting God by something else or simply god not God.

Reincarnation = the recycling of the soul after the body is dead. This is not a church teaching.

Relativism = means every knowledge or idea is relative and not absolute. For example, there is no right and no wrong, no moral or immoral-what is right for one could be wrong for others.

Agnostic = no knowledge of God or no idea of God, but agnosticism is still a form of atheism and is widely used as a euphemistic word for atheism.

Anti-Semitism = modern-day definition for hate of the Jews or anything Jewish in any form open or disguised.

Abortion and euthanasia = assisted termination of life is not Christian practice because life is sacred (sanctified) from 'conception to natural death'.

Unitarianism = is a belief in God only and the rejection of the Trinitarian God (Father, Son and Holy Spirit). Unitarianism goes back to the times of the early Church when orthodox Christianity prevailed and Unitarianism of Arius of Alexandria was rejected in the fourth century. Arius rejected the deity of Jesus or that Jesus is consubstantial with the Father.

Humanism = or secular humanism is to place humanity or humans or human reason at the centre of the society as opposed to Christianity which places God at the centre.

Secular humanism opts for gradual diminution of Christianity or de-Christianisation of the society and promotion of a society based on human secular principles.

Globalisation = is to create a kingdom of man based on one-world government, one-world culture and one-world economic system as opposed to God's Kingdom. Global is not international and is opposed to national. Globalisation is a pipedream to solve humanity's problems.

Post-Christianity = a term used in Western Europe to indicate that the West after World War I and II due to their consequences, it is no longer Christian but instead adheres to secularism, nationalism, socialism or even Marxism. For example, the European Union's charter does not mention Christianity at all.

Political correctness = also called 'identity politics' is to go with the flow (here is labelled correct) even when the flow is incorrect. Do not say something that may offend others even when it is right in saying it. Political incorrectness is the opposite.

Multicultural = is a modern invention in the West and means immigrants can keep their culture without being required to integrate into the existing society. This proved to be unworkable.

Liberal = means not bound by tradition and conservative values and open or tolerant of anything or others whatever the consequences.

Paganism = or pagan is the worship of nature-the universe is god or gods.

Universalism = everyone will be saved.

Pluralism = all religions lead to God.

Occult = satanic rituals.

Cult = a confined and dominated culture or a 'hidden manipulation'.

Barbarian = old definition for someone who is neither Greek nor Roman (Latin).

New Age = as a movement it surfaced in the West in the 1970s and 1980s. It teaches an individual to search for the missing meaning of life that sets the individual free. It negates the existence of any divine nature and believes in aliens' connection and the practise of yoga and meditation to gain pure consciousness and power to even become a god.

Eugenics = is human manipulation in 'human mating' for the purpose of better 'hereditary qualities' by genetic means or other unethical means. Christianity regards eugenics as evil.

Determinism or Fatalism=means there is no free will and every action is already determined and cannot be changed. This is not a church teaching.

Intelligent Design = does not mean God created the heavens and the earth but there is an intentional design in nature not an evolved nature.

Freedom of religion = full freedom for practising the faith without hindrance or interference.

Freedom of worship = limited freedom for practising the faith, for example, the church in the Middle East.

Hate speech = is speech or writing against specified race, religion, culture etc. But hate speech can be used to silence the church, for example when the church says marriage is between a man and a woman, it can be considered a hate speech. Or when we say Jesus is the only mediator between man and God, it can also be considered a hate speech.

Personal Notes
How to Read the Bible?

In the early 1970s, I had bought my first copy of the Holy Bible written in the language of the land. I tried to read it from cover to cover i.e. from Genesis to Revelation but I have failed to continue. It was hard.

In the late 1970s and early 1980s I have tried again reading the Bible but through handpicked chapters and books and that made me enjoy it and this time I have succeeded. I went through some Gospels, Acts, Psalms and Isaiah.

In 1983, I bought my own copy of the Holy Bible (NIV version) and it is still my precious Bible. The NIV version was the most read version at the time. In 1992, I was determined to read it from cover to cover so I did and it has taken me about seven years to finish the reading but with a deep understanding and many times repeating the verse or verses until I was satisfied with the meaning.

I have spent another one to two years reading the books of Apocrypha but using The Good News Bible. My third Bible is King James Version and it is advisable as I have learned to have more than one authorised version and use the one you like most.

In late 2013, I have started reading the Bible from cover to cover for the third time and I have committed myself reading the Bible until my life on earth is over.

Note: Read the Holy Bible from cover to cover slowly in most parts of it but faster in some parts of the Old Testaments that elaborate about description, listing, measurement and counting.

My final remark is that a Christian cannot be a churchgoer only but must either be an evangelist or witness. An Evangelist is the one who takes the gospel to his neighbour (means anyone) and this is the highest Biblical outreach.

Evangelisation is a direct preaching and spreading of the Gospel of Jesus Christ to people or nations through convocations, street evangelism, education programmes, health programmes, humanitarian programmes, radio and television. In other words, it is making disciples by all possible means.

The lower approach is Christian witnessing in that you show or share your Christian beliefs with other non-Christian individuals through personality, demeanour and deed. For example, when seeing or contacting someone you should show a Christian character and when someone enters your house the person must feel he/she is in Christian milieu.

The Core New Testament Verses

These are the core verses selected from the New Testament. Few more verses were already given above:

"For there is one God and one mediator between God and men, the man Christ Jesus, who gave himself as a ransom for all men..." (1Timothy 2:5–6).

"My I never boast except in the cross of our Lord Jesus Christ, through which the world has been crucified to me, and I to the world." (Galatians 6:14).

"For Christ died for sins once for all, the righteous for the unrighteous, to bring you to God..." (1 Peter 3:18).

"There is neither Jew nor Greek, slave nor free, male nor female, for you are all one in Christ Jesus." (Galatians 3:28).

"For it is by grace you have been saved, through faith…" (Ephesians 2:8).

"As the body without the spirit is dead, so faith without deeds is dead." (James 2:26).

"…the one who is in you is greater than the one who is in the world." (1 John 4:4).

"Therefore, if anyone is in Christ, he is a new creation; the old has gone, the new has come!" (2 Corinthians 5:17).

"I have been crucified with Christ and I no longer live, but Christ lives in me. The life I live in the body, I live by faith in the Son of God, who loved me and gave himself for me." (Galatians 2:20).

"May the grace of the Lord Jesus Christ, and the love of God, and the fellowship of the Holy Spirit be with you all." (2 Corinthians 13:13).

"Here I am! I stand at the door and knock…" (Revelation 3.20).

"Behold, I am coming soon!" (Revelation 22:7).

"For I am already being poured out like a drink offering, and the time has come for my departure. I have fought the good fight, I have finished the race, I have kept the faith." (2 Timothy 4:6–7).